MENSA
Number
Puzzles
for Kids

No part of this publication may be reproduced in whole
or in part, or stored in a retrieval system, or transmitted
in any form or by any means, electronic, mechanical,
photocopying, recording, or otherwise, without written
permission of the publisher. For information regarding
permission, write to Carlton Books Limited,
14 Soho Square, London, England.

ISBN 0-439-10841-1

Text and puzzle content copyright © 1994 and 1997
by British Mensa Limited.
Design and artwork copyright © 1994 and 1997
by Carlton Books Limited.
All rights reserved.
Published by Scholastic Inc., 555 Broadway, New York,
NY 10012, by arrangement with Carlton Books Limited.
SCHOLASTIC and associated logos are trademarks
and/or registered trademarks of Scholastic Inc.

12 11 10 9 8 7 6   3 4/0

Printed in the U.S.A.   01

First Scholastic printing, September 1999

MENSA
Number
Puzzles
for Kids

Harold Gale & Carolyn Skitt

SCHOLASTIC INC.

New York Toronto London Auckland Sydney
Mexico City New Delhi Hong Kong

INTRODUCTION

Welcome to the world of numbers! In this book you will meet dinosaurs, zap spaceships and count coins from the distant planet of Venox. In fact, you'll have all sorts of weird and wonderful adventures. There are unusual boxes to be made, animals to trace through and flags with a difference. These puzzles, along with many, many others, will give you hours of pleasure — and that's not all. The more you use your brain, the sharper it will become! So as you work your way through the six different levels, you will find yourself becoming smarter and smarter! Think of how pleased you will be with yourself when you can solve puzzles that you thought were impossible.

Good luck and have fun!

How To Join
MENSA

If you like puzzles, then you'll like Mensa. It is the only club that lets you in just because you are good at puzzling. Mensa has 120,000 members throughout the world (with the majority in the USA and Great Britain). The great thing about Mensa is that you get to meet so many people with different interests. For more information about American Mensa, you can write to American Mensa Ltd., 1229 Corporate Drive West, Arlington, TX 76006-6103.

EASY DOES IT

PUZZLE 1

Using the numbers shown how many different ways are there to add three numbers together to make a total of 8? A number can be used more than once, but a group cannot be repeated in a different order?

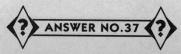

ANSWER NO. 37

PUZZLE 2

Move up or across from the bottom left-hand 1 to the top right-hand 1. Collect nine numbers and add them together. What is the highest you can score?

EASY DOES IT

A

1	1	2	1	1
1	2	2	1	2
1	1	1	1	1
1	1	1	2	1
1	1	1	1	2

◆ ANSWER NO. 169 ◆

PUZZLE 3

Join together the dots using odd numbers only.
Start at the lowest and discover the object. What is it?

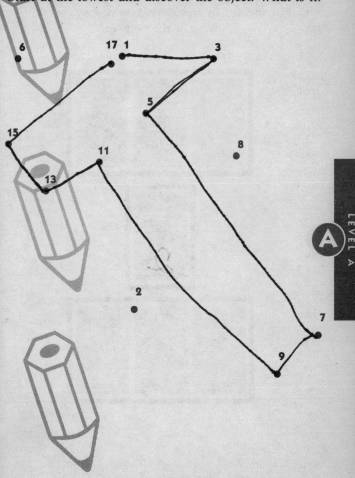

LEVEL A

A Hammer
ANSWER NO.122

PUZZLE 4

Place in the middle box a number larger than 1.
If the number is the correct one, all the other numbers
can be divided by it without leaving any remainder.
What is the number?

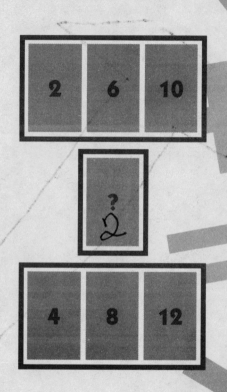

ANSWER NO.73

PUZZLE 5

Each sector of the circle follows a pattern.
What number should replace the question mark?

LEVEL A

? ANSWER NO.145 ?

PUZZLE 6

Here is an unusual safe. Each of the buttons must be pressed only once in the correct order to open it. The last button is marked F. The number of moves and the direction is marked on each button. Thus 1U would mean one move up, whilst 1L would mean one move to the left. Which button is the first you must press? Here's a clue: it can be found on the top row.

F	3R	2D	2R	1L	2D
1U	1L	2D	2R	1L	3L
1R	2U	1R	1D	4L	1D
1D	3R	1D	2L	2U	5L
3R	3U	3R	2L	2U	1L

ANSWER NO.26

PUZZLE 7

Each slice of this cake adds up to the same number.
What number should replace the question mark?

PUZZLE 8

Copy out these shapes carefully and rearrange them
to form a number. What is it?

EASY DOES IT

PUZZLE 9

If you look carefully you should see why the numbers are written as they are. What number should replace the question mark?

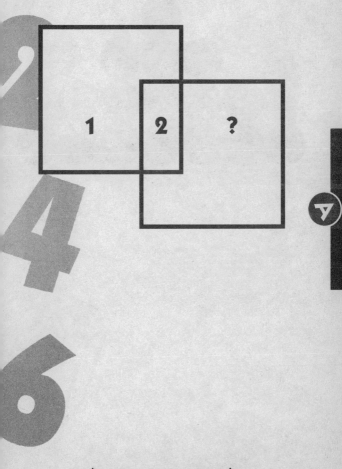

LEVEL A

ANSWER NO. 14

PUZZLE 10

Look at the pattern of numbers in the diagram.
What number should replace the question mark?

PUZZLE 11

Move from the bottom left-hand 3 to the top right-hand 3 adding together all five numbers. Each black circle is worth 1 and this should be added to your total each time you meet one. What is the highest total you can find?

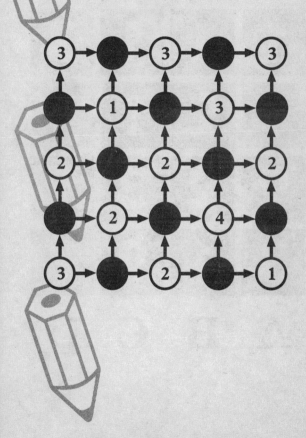

LEVEL A

? ANSWER NO.85 ?

PUZZLE 12

The numbers in column D are linked in some way to those in A, B and C. What number should replace the question mark?

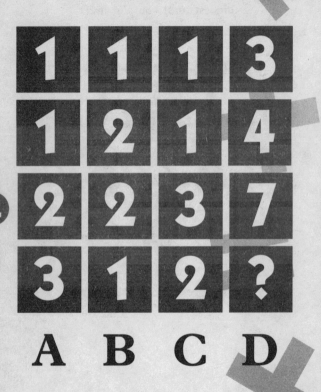

A   B   C   D

ANSWER NO.133

PUZZLE 13

Start at the A and move to B passing through various
parts of the rhinoceros. There is a number in each
part and these must be added together.
What is the lowest number you can total?

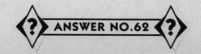

ANSWER NO.62

PUZZLE 14

Each symbol is worth a number. The total of the
symbols can be found alongside each row. What
number should replace the question mark?

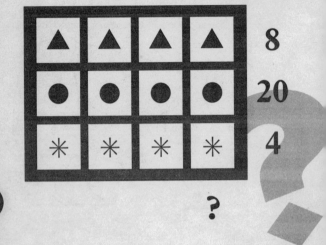

?

PUZZLE 15

On the planet Venox the coins used are 1V, 2V, 5V, 10V, 20V and 50V. A Venoxian has 85V in his squiggly bank. He has the same number of three kinds of coin. How many of each are there and what are they?

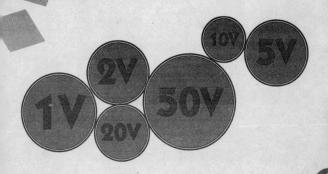

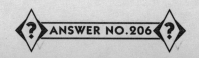

ANSWER NO.206

PUZZLE 16

What is the lowest number of lines needed to divide the camel so that you can find the numbers 1, 2 and 3 in each selection?

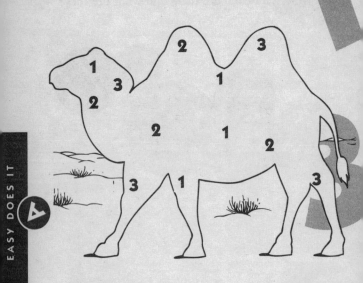

ANSWER NO.98

PUZZLE 17

Fill up this square with the numbers 1 to 5 so that no row, column or diagonal line of five squares uses the same number more than once. What number should replace the question mark?

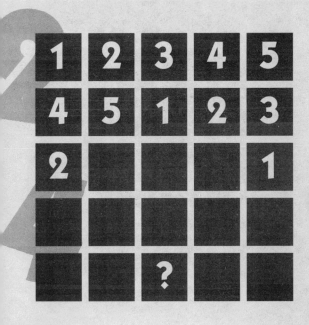

PUZZLE 18

Follow the arrows and find the longest possible route.
How many boxes have been entered?

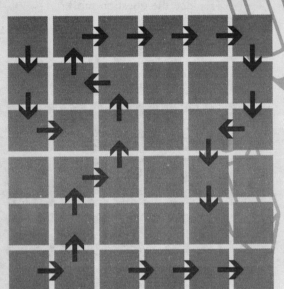

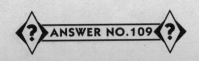

ANSWER NO.109

PUZZLE 19

The symbol on the flag will give a number. What is it?

LEVEL A

? ANSWER NO.146 **?**

PUZZLE 20

Start at the middle 3 and move from circle to touching circle. Collect three numbers and add them to the 3. How many different routes are there to make a total of 8?

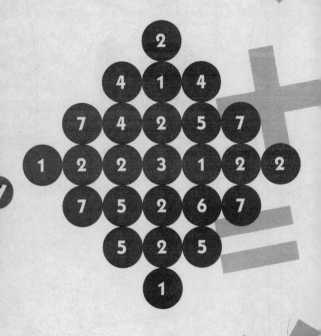

PUZZLE 21

How many squares of any size can you find in this diagram?

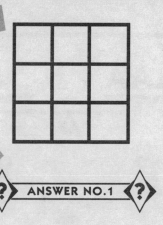

ANSWER NO.1

PUZZLE 22

Turn the number shown on the calculator into 32 by pressing two buttons only. What are they?

ANSWER NO.86

PUZZLE 23

The first set of scales balance.
How many A's will make the second set balance?

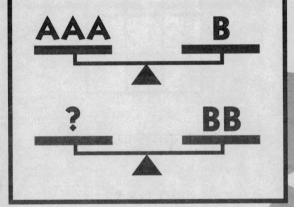

ANSWER NO. 121

PUZZLE 24

Divide up the box using four lines so that each shape adds up to the same. How is this done?

2	5	5	9
8	9	2	5
5	8	9	2
9	2	8	8

LEVEL A

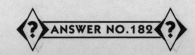

PUZZLE 25

Which squares contain the same numbers?

	A	B	C	D
1	3 6	7 6	5 4	2 2
2	6 2	3 2	2 1	5 1
3	1 1	5 5	6 3	6 6
4	4 1	5 3	3 4	3 3

ANSWER NO.134

EASY DOES IT

PUZZLE 26

Fill in the empty boxes so that every line adds up to 5, including the lines that go from corner to corner. What number should replace the question mark?

1	2	1	0	
1	1	1		1
0	1	?		2
1	0	1		1

LEVEL A

ANSWER NO.61

PUZZLE 27

Copy out these shapes carefully and rearrange them to form a number. What is it?

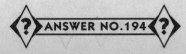
ANSWER NO.194

PUZZLE 28

Which number should be placed in the triangle to continue the series?

 ANSWER NO.38

PUZZLE 29

Here is a series of numbers. Which number should replace the question mark?

LEVEL A

 ANSWER NO.193

PUZZLE 30

Replace each question mark with either plus, minus, multiply or divide. Each sign can be used more than once. When the correct ones have been used the sum will be completed. What are the signs?

| 1 | ? | 1 | ? | 3 | = | 5 |

ANSWER NO.97

PUZZLE 31

How many 3's can be found in this Pterodactyl?

ANSWER NO.158

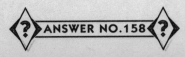

PUZZLE 32

Which of these pictures is not of the same box?

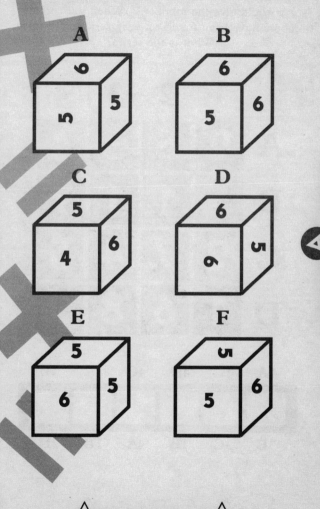

A

B

C

D

E

F

ANSWER NO.110

LEVEL A

PUZZLE 33

Find the correct six numbers to put in the frame.
There are two choices for each square, for example
1A would give the number 2. When the correct
numbers have been found an easy series will appear.
What is the series?

	1	2	3	4
A	2	5	3	4
B	5	1	1	7
C	2	7	4	5
D	1	6	8	3

1A	1C	4D	4C	2A	4B
3B	3C	1B	4A	1D	2D

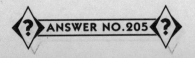

ANSWER NO.205

PUZZLE 34

The numbers in the middle section have some connection with those down the sides. Find out what it is and tell us what should replace the question mark?

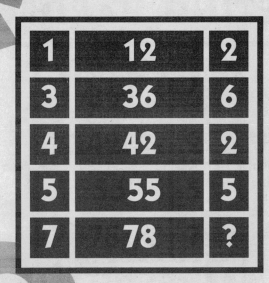

1	12	2
3	36	6
4	42	2
5	55	5
7	78	?

LEVEL A

? ANSWER NO.2 ?

B

GETING HARDER

★ LEVEL B ★

PUZZLE 35

The numbers in the middle section have some
connection with those down the sides.
Find out what it is and tell us what should replace
the question mark?

3	23	2
1	61	6
7	47	4
5	35	3
9	?	1

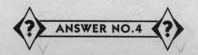

ANSWER NO.4

PUZZLE 36

Which number should be placed in the triangle to continue the series?

ANSWER NO.40

PUZZLE 37

Copy the cake slices out carefully and rearrange them to find the birthday. How old was the birthday boy?

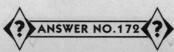
ANSWER NO.172

PUZZLE 38

Zap the spaceship by making its number a round one. Take off either 11, 13, 19, 21 or 25 to do this. Which number ought you to use?

ANSWER NO.76

GETTING HARDER

B

PUZZLE 39

Move up or across from the bottom left-hand 2 to the top right-hand 1. Collect nine numbers and add them together. What is the highest you can score?

PUZZLE 40

Start at any corner and follow the lines. Add up the
first four numbers you meet and then add on the
corner number. What is the lowest you can score?

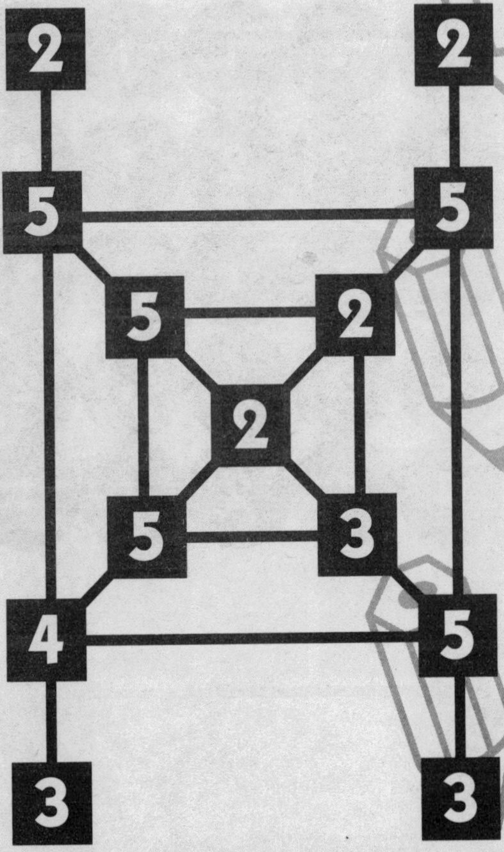

GETTING HARDER

B

ANSWER NO.51

PUZZLE 41

Place in the middle box a number larger than 1.
If the number is the correct one, all the other numbers
can be divided by it without leaving any remainder.
What is the number?

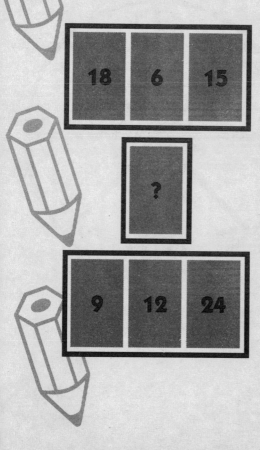

? ANSWER NO. 75 ?

PUZZLE 42

Each sector of the circle follows a pattern.
What number should replace the question mark?

ANSWER NO.147

PUZZLE 43

Each slice of this cake adds up to the same number.
All the numbers going round the cake total 24.
Which two numbers should appear on the blank slice?

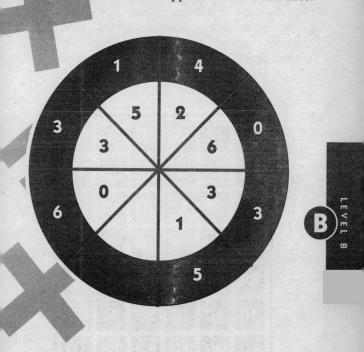

ANSWER NO. 15

LEVEL B

B

PUZZLE 44

Here is an unusual safe. Each of the buttons must be
pressed only once in the correct order to open it. The
last button is marked F. The number of moves and
the direction is marked on each button. Thus 1U
would mean one move up, whilst 1L would
mean one move to the left. Which button is the first
you must press? Here's a clue: it can be found on the
middle row.

GETTING HARDER

B

F	4R	2R	1D	4D	6D
1U	4R	1D	1L	5D	1D
3R	3R	1L	2D	1D	5L
3D	2U	1R	3D	3L	5L
2R	4U	1D	2R	3U	5L
1R	1D	1D	5U	4L	2U
5U	2U	6U	1U	1U	1U

? ANSWER NO.28 ?

PUZZLE 45

If you look carefully you should see why the numbers are written as they are. What number should replace the question mark?

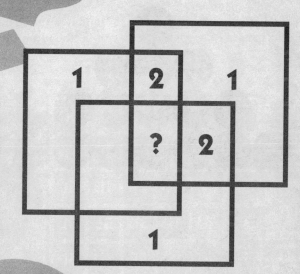

LEVEL B

B

PUZZLE 46

Look at the pattern of numbers in the diagram.
What number should replace the question mark?

◇? ANSWER NO.159 ?◇

GETTING HARDER

B

PUZZLE 47

Start at the A and move to B passing through the various parts of the cat. There is a number in each part and these must be added together.
What is the lowest number you can total?

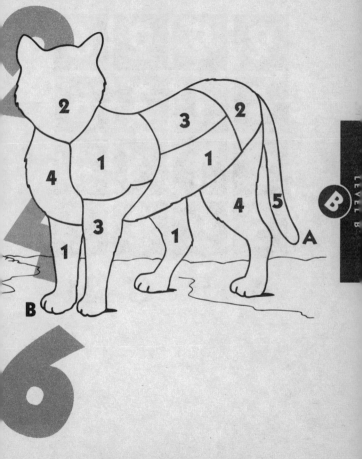

ANSWER NO.64

PUZZLE 48

The numbers in column D are linked in some way to those in A, B and C. What number should replace the question mark?

A B C D

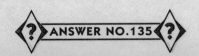

PUZZLE 49

Move from the bottom left-hand 5 to the top right-hand 2 adding together all five numbers. Each black circle is worth 2 and this should be added to your total each time you meet one. What is the highest total you can find?

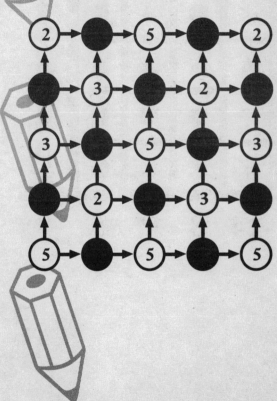

B

ANSWER NO.87

PUZZLE 50

Each symbol is worth a number. The total of the symbols can be found alongside each row and column. What number should replace the question mark?

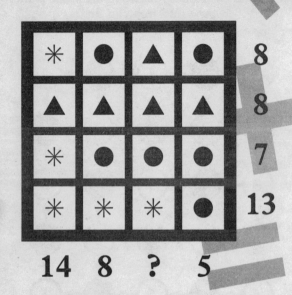

PUZZLE 51

On the planet Venox the coins used are 1V, 2V, 5V, 10V, 20V and 50V. A Venoxian has 374V in his squiggly bank. He has the same number of three kinds of coin. How many of each are there and what are they?

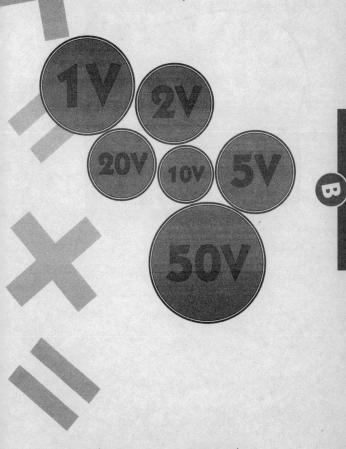

ANSWER NO.208

PUZZLE 52

What is the lowest number of lines needed to divide the elephant so that you can find the numbers 1, 2, 3 and 4 in each section?

PUZZLE 53

Here is a series of numbers. Which number should replace the question mark?

| 4 | 8 | 12 | 16 | 20 | 24 | ? |

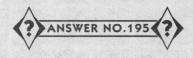

ANSWER NO.195

PUZZLE 54

Replace each question mark with either plus, minus, multiply or divide. Each sign can be used more than once. When the correct ones have been used the sum will be completed. What are the signs?

| 2 | ? | 3 | ? | 1 | | = | 4 |

LEVEL B

ANSWER NO.99

PUZZLE 55

Follow the arrows and find the longest possible route.
How many boxes have been entered?

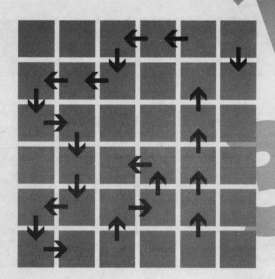

◇ ANSWER NO.111 ◇

PUZZLE 56

The symbol on the flag will give a number. What is it?

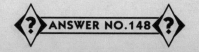ANSWER NO.148

PUZZLE 57

Start at the middle 1 and move from circle to touching circle. Collect three numbers and add them to the 1. How many different routes are there to make a total of 10?

ANSWER NO.27

PUZZLE 58

How many squares of any size can you find in this diagram?

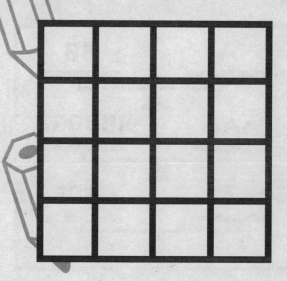

LEVEL B

? ANSWER NO.3 ?

PUZZLE 59

Scales 1 and 2 are in perfect balance.
How many A's are needed to balance the third set?

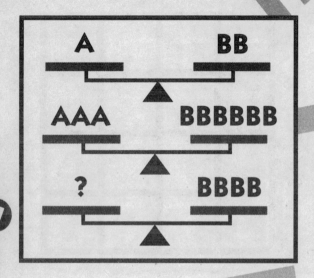

B

◇ ANSWER NO.123 ◇

PUZZLE 60

Divide up the box into four identical shapes. The
numbers in each shape add up to the same.
How is this done?

LEVEL B

‹?›ANSWER NO. 184‹?›

PUZZLE 61

Which squares contain the same numbers?

	A	B	C	D
1	4 1 / 1	5 / 2 1	2 2 / 1	4 / 1 3
2	3 / 3 / 3	4 5 4	3 / 5 5	1 1 / 1 4
3	2 5 / 3	1 / 3 2	3 4 / 3	4 / 1 2
4	2 / 1 1	4 4 4	1 4 5	1 / 2 5

ANSWER NO. 136

PUZZLE 62

Which buttons must be used to produce the number on the calculator? Only three buttons can be used.

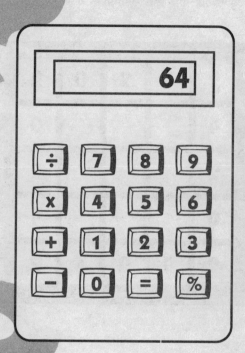

ANSWER NO.88

PUZZLE 63

Fill in the empty boxes so that every line adds up to 10, including the lines that go from corner to corner, using only one number. What is it?

2	4	2	0	2
4				0
2				2
0				4
2	0	2	4	2

◆? ANSWER NO.63 ?◆

PUZZLE 64

Copy the cake slices out carefully and rearrange them to find the birthday. How old was the birthday girl?

ANSWER NO. 170

B

PUZZLE 65

Join together the dots using odd numbers only. Start at the lowest and discover the object. What is it?

15

23 17   2

14

13

19

25

18   11 21   30

PUZZLE 66

Which of these pictures is not of the same box?

A

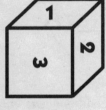

B

C

D

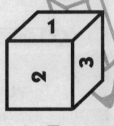

E

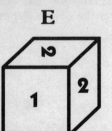

F

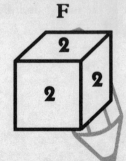

ANSWER NO.112

PUZZLE 67

Fill up this square with the numbers 1 to 5 so that no row, column or diagonal line of five squares uses the same number more than once. What number should replace the question mark?

1	2	3	4	5
4		1		
		4		
		2		
		5		?

LEVEL B

PUZZLE 68

How many 5s can be found in this mammoth?

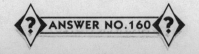ANSWER NO. 160

GETTING HARDER

B

PUZZLE 69

Find the correct six numbers to put in the frame.
There are two choices for each square, for example
1A would give the number 12. When the correct
numbers have been found an easy series will appear.
What is the series?

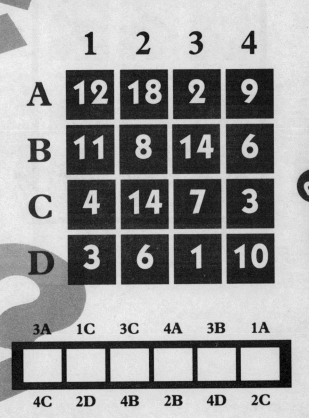

	1	2	3	4
A	12	18	2	9
B	11	8	14	6
C	4	14	7	3
D	3	6	1	10

3A	1C	3C	4A	3B	1A
4C	2D	4B	2B	4D	2C

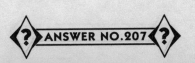

ANSWER NO.207

PUZZLE 70

Which of the numbers in the square is the odd one out and why?

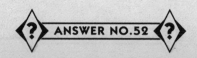

ANSWER NO. 52

PUZZLE 71

Using the numbers shown how many different ways are there to add three numbers together to make a total of 10? A number can be used more than once, but a group cannot be repeated in a different order?

LEVEL B

ANSWER NO.39

C

FIENDISH FIGURES

★ LEVEL C ★

PUZZLE 72

The numbers in the middle section have some connection with those down the sides. Find out what it is and tell us what should replace the question mark?

5	10	5
2	9	7
8	12	4
3	6	3
5	?	6

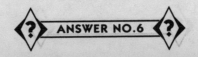

ANSWER NO.6

PUZZLE 73

Move up or across from the bottom left-hand 3 to the top right-hand 3. Collect nine numbers and add them together. What is the lowest you can score?

ANSWER NO.175

PUZZLE 74

Start at any corner and follow the lines. Add up the first four numbers you meet and then add on the corner number. What is the highest you can score?

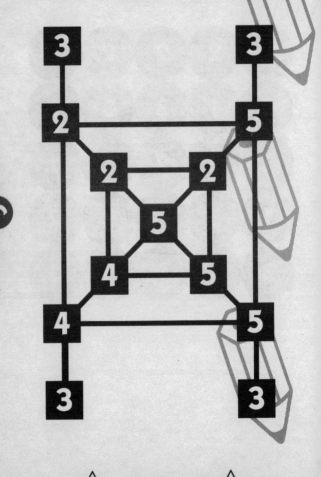

ANSWER NO.53

PUZZLE 75

Place in the middle box a number larger than 1.
If the number is the correct one, all the other numbers
can be divided by it without leaving any remainder.
What is the number?

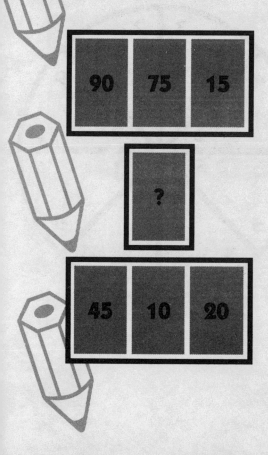

90	75	15

?

45	10	20

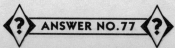

ANSWER NO.77

PUZZLE 76

Each sector of the circle follows a pattern.
What number should replace the question mark?

ANSWER NO. 149

PUZZLE 77

Copy out these shapes carefully and rearrange them to form a number. What is it?

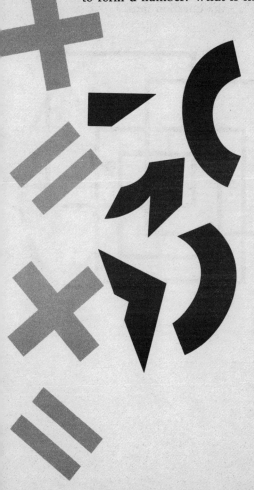

PUZZLE 78

If you look carefully you should see why the numbers are written as they are. What number should replace the question mark?

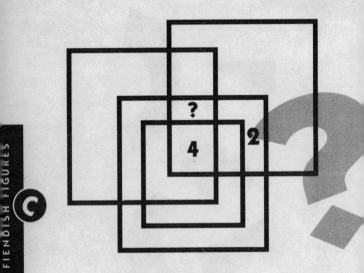

ANSWER NO. 18

PUZZLE 79

Each slice of this cake adds up to the same number.
All the numbers going round the cake total 32.
Which numbers should appear in the blanks?

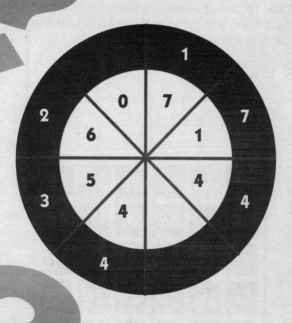

LEVEL C

ANSWER NO.17

PUZZLE 80

Here is an unusual safe. Each of the buttons must be pressed only once in the correct order to open it. The last button is marked F. The number of moves and the direction is marked on each button. Thus 1N would mean one move north, whilst 1W would mean one move to the west. Which button is the first you must press? Here's a clue: it can be found on the middle row.

F	4E	1S	6S	2W	6S
5S	1N	1E	2E	4W	2S
4E	1W	3E	2N	4S	2W
2E	1W	1S	2S	3W	2S
1E	3N	2N	2E	1N	1W
1N	3N	2E	1N	5N	5W
6N	1N	1N	1W	5N	4W

ANSWER NO.30

PUZZLE 81

Look at each line of numbers in the diagram.
What number should replace the question mark?

LEVEL C

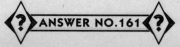

ANSWER NO.161

PUZZLE 82

On the planet Venox the coins used are 1V, 2V, 5V, 10V, 20V and 50V. A Venoxian has 306V in his squiggly bank. He has the same number of four kinds of coin. How many of each are there and what are they?

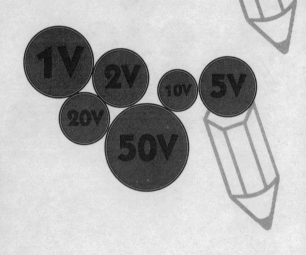

PUZZLE 83

Start at the A and move to B passing through the various parts of the horse. There is a number in each part and these must be added together.
What is the lowest number you can total?

PUZZLE 84

The numbers in column D are linked in some way to those in A, B and C. What number should replace the question mark?

A	B	C	D
5	3	1	9
4	2	2	8
3	1	4	8
1	5	1	?

A B C D

ANSWER NO. 137

PUZZLE 85

Move from the bottom left-hand 4 to the top right-hand 3 adding together all five numbers. Each black circle is worth minus 1 and this should be taken away from your total each time you meet one. What is the highest total you can find?

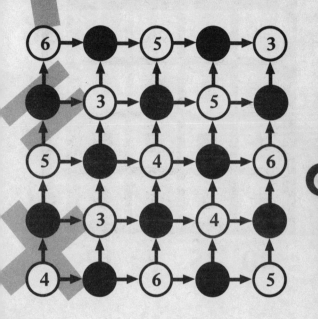

◆ ANSWER NO.89 ◆

PUZZLE 86

Each symbol is worth a number. The total of the symbols can be found alongside each row and column. What number should replace the question mark?

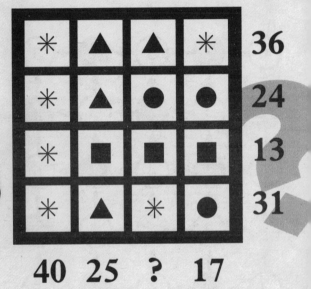

ANSWER NO.185

PUZZLE 87

What is the lowest number of lines needed to divide
the rhinoceros so that you can find the numbers
1, 2, 3, 4 and 5 in each section?

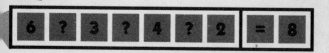
ANSWER NO.102

LEVEL C

PUZZLE 88

Replace each question mark with either plus, minus,
multiply or divide. Each sign can be used more than
once. When the correct ones have been used
the sum will be completed. What are the signs?

| 6 | ? | 3 | ? | 4 | ? | 2 | = | 8 |

ANSWER NO.101

PUZZLE 89

Follow the arrows and find the longest possible route. How many boxes have been entered?

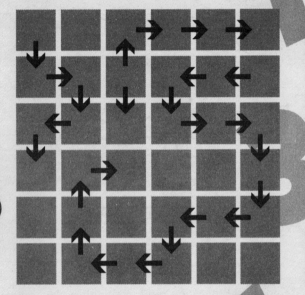

ANSWER NO.113

PUZZLE 90

The symbol on the flag will give a number. What is it?

ANSWER NO.150

PUZZLE 91

Start at the middle 2 and move from circle to touching circle. Collect three numbers and add them to the 2. How many different routes are there to make a total of 12?

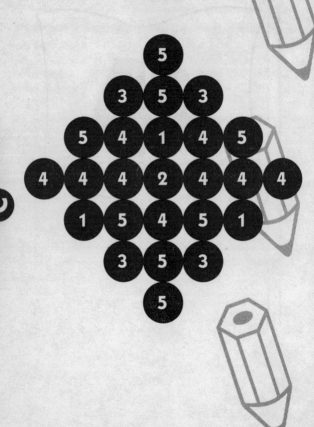

ANSWER NO.29

PUZZLE 92

Divide up the box using four lines so that each shape adds up to the same. How is this done?

1	6	1	2	4
6	6	4	6	1
2	4	2	1	6
4	2	6	6	2
6	1	6	4	6

ANSWER NO. 186

PUZZLE 93

Scales 1 and 2 are in perfect balance. If one C is the same as four As, how many As are needed to balance the third set?

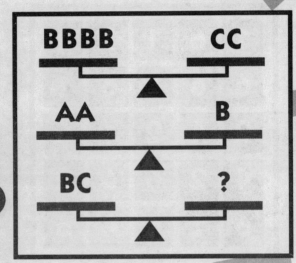

ANSWER NO.125

PUZZLE 94

How many rectangles of any size can you find in this diagram? Remember a square is also a rectangle!

ANSWER NO.5

PUZZLE 95

Which number should replace the question mark to continue the series?

9   **10**   **11**   **12**

1   5   2   ?   3   7   4   8

ANSWER NO.42

PUZZLE 96

Which squares contain the same numbers?

	A	B	C	D
1	2 3 1	1 3 1	2 1 2	1 3 6
2	4 2 4	6 4 5	2 2 2	3 4 2
3	3 3 4	6 3 1	5 6 5	1 1 1
4	3 3 3	2 4 2	3 4 1	5 5 5

ANSWER NO.138

PUZZLE 97

One two-digit number should be used to divide the one shown on the calculator to get the answer 11. What is the number?

LEVEL C

? ANSWER NO.90 ?

PUZZLE 98

Fill in the empty boxes so that every line adds up to the same, including the lines that go from corner to corner. Which two numbers will be used to do this?

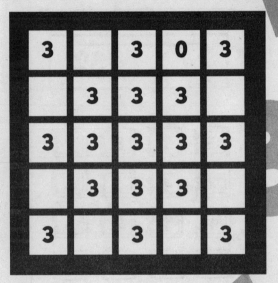

PUZZLE 99

Copy the cake slices out carefully and rearrange them to find the birthday. How old was the birthday boy?

? ANSWER NO.174 ?

PUZZLE 100

Zap the spaceship by finding a one-didgit number which will divide without remainder all the numbers which appear on it. Which number ought you to use?

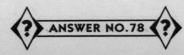

ANSWER NO.78

PUZZLE 101

Here is a series of numbers.
Which number should replace the question mark?

| 1 | 4 | 7 | 10 | 13 | ? | 19 |

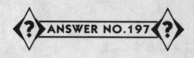

ANSWER NO.197

PUZZLE 102

Join together the dots using even numbers
only. Start at the lowest and discover the object.
What is it?

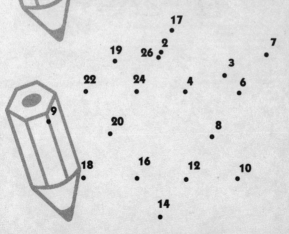

LEVEL C

ANSWER NO.126

PUZZLE 103

How many 4s can be found in this stegosaurus?

FIENDISH FIGURES

ANSWER NO.162

PUZZLE 104

Find the correct six numbers to put in the frame.
There are two choices for each square, for example
1A would give the number 9. When the correct
numbers have been found an easy series will appear.
What is the series?

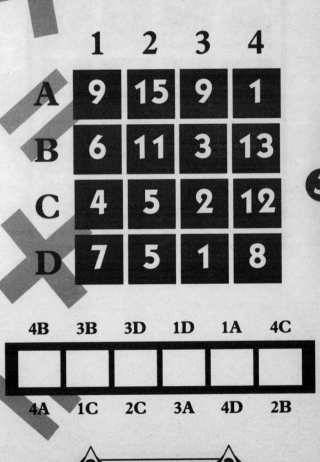

	1	2	3	4
A	9	15	9	1
B	6	11	3	13
C	4	5	2	12
D	7	5	1	8

4B	3B	3D	1D	1A	4C
4A	1C	2C	3A	4D	2B

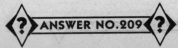

◆ ? ANSWER NO.209 ? ◆

PUZZLE 105

Which of the numbers in the square is the odd one out and why?

41	7	33	13
21	27	32	63
9	49	3	25
17	29	57	1

◆ **ANSWER NO. 54** ◆

PUZZLE 106

Each slice of this cake has a number written on it.
Using the numbers shown how many different ways
are there to add three numbers together to make a
total of 13? A number can be used more than once,
but a group cannot be repeated in a different order.

ANSWER NO.41

PUZZLE 107

Which of these pictures is not of the same box?

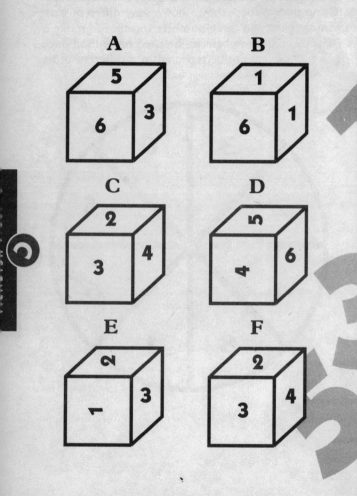

? ANSWER NO.114 ?

PUZZLE 108

Fill up this square with the numbers 1 to 5 so that no row, column or diagonal line of five squares uses the same number more than once. What number should replace the question mark?

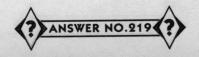ANSWER NO.219

PUZZLE 109

Move up or across from the bottom left-hand 5 to the top right-hand 5. Collect nine numbers and add them together. What is the highest you can score?

◆? ANSWER NO.49 ?◆

MIND NUMBING

★ LEVEL D ★

PUZZLE 110

The numbers in the middle section have some connection with those down the sides. Find out what it is and tell us what should replace the question mark?

8	4	4
3	1	2
7	2	5
6	5	1
9	?	3

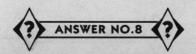
ANSWER NO. 8

PUZZLE 111

Move up or across from the bottom left-hand 2 to the top right-hand 3. Collect nine numbers and add them together. What is the highest you can score?

ANSWER NO.173

PUZZLE 112

Start at any corner and follow the lines. Add up the
first four numbers you meet and then add on the
corner number. What is the highest you can score?

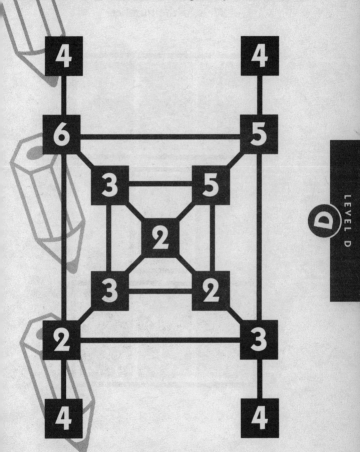

ANSWER NO.55

PUZZLE 113

Place in the middle box a number larger than 1.
If the number is the correct one, all the other numbers
can be divided by it without leaving any remainder.
What is the number?

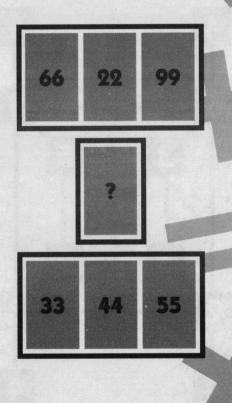

66	22	99

?

33	44	55

ANSWER NO.79

PUZZLE 114

Each sector of the circle follows a pattern.
What number should replace the question mark?

LEVEL D

PUZZLE 115

Here is an unusual safe. Each of the buttons must be pressed only once in the correct order to open it. The last button is marked F. The number of moves and the direction is marked on each button. Thus 1i would mean one move in, whilst 1O would mean one move out. 1C would mean one move clockwise and 1A would mean one move anti-clockwise. Which button is the first you must press? Here's a clue: look around the outer rim.

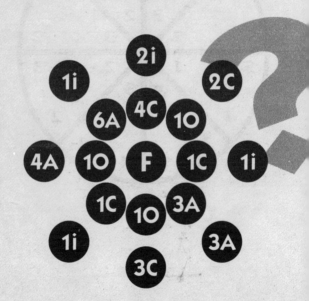

PUZZLE 116

Each slice of this cake adds up to the same number.
Also each ring of the cake totals the same.
Which number should appear in the blanks?

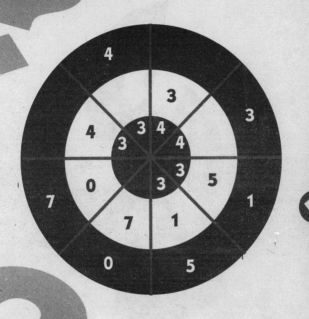

LEVEL D

ANSWER NO.19

PUZZLE 117

Copy the cake slices out carefully and rearrange them to find the birthday. How old was the birthday boy?

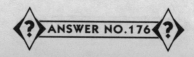
ANSWER NO.176

PUZZLE 118

If you look carefully you should see why the
numbers are written as they are.
What number should replace the question mark?

PUZZLE 119

Start at the A and move to B passing through various parts of the elephant. There is a number in each part and these must be added together.
What is the lowest number you can total?

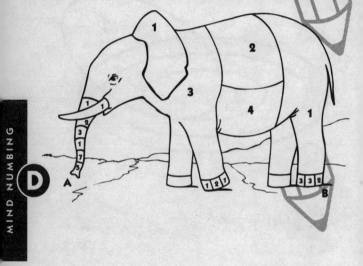

ANSWER NO.68

PUZZLE 120

Move from the bottom left-hand 5 to the top right-hand 4 adding together all five numbers. Each black circle is worth minus 3 and this should be taken away from your total each time you meet one. What is the highest total you can find?

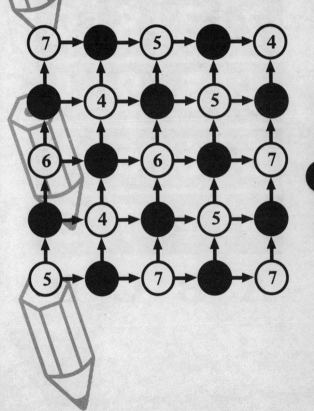

LEVEL D

D

◇ ANSWER NO.91 ◇

PUZZLE 121

The numbers in column D are linked in some way to those in A, B and C. What number should replace the question mark?

A	B	C	D
7	3	8	2
1	5	2	4
6	6	6	?
9	1	7	3

PUZZLE 122

Each symbol is worth a number. The total of the symbols can be found alongside each row and column. What number should replace the question mark?

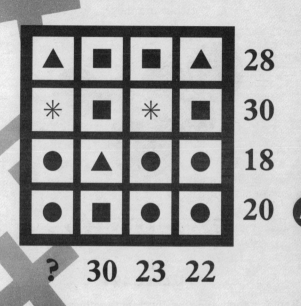

28
30
18
20

? 30 23 22

L E V E L   D

D

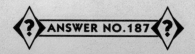

ANSWER NO. 187

PUZZLE 123

On the planet Venox the coins used are 1V, 2V, 5V,
10V, 20V and 50V. A Venoxian has 558V in his
squiggly bank. He has the same number of four kinds
of coin. How many of each are there and
what are they?

ANSWER NO.212

PUZZLE 124

Replace each question mark with either plus, minus,
multiply or divide. Each sign can be used more than
once. When the correct ones have been used
the sum will be completed. What are the signs?

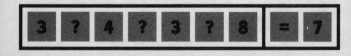

ANSWER NO.103

PUZZLE 125

What is the lowest number of lines needed to divide the reindeer so that you can find the numbers 1, 2, 3, 4 and 5 in each section?

? ANSWER NO.104 ?

PUZZLE 126

Follow the arrows and find the longest possible route.
How many boxes have been entered?

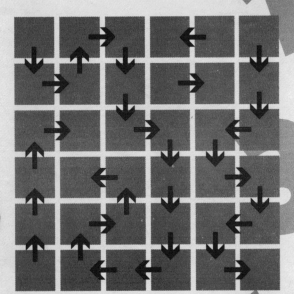

◆ ANSWER NO.115 ◆

PUZZLE 127

The symbol on the flag will give a number. What is it?

PUZZLE 128

Start at the middle 7 and move from circle to touching circle. Collect three numbers and add them to the 7. How many different routes are there to make a total of 20?

PUZZLE 129

Divide up the box into four identical shapes.
The numbers in each shape add up to the same.
How is this done?

9	8	4	3
3	5	8	5
4	4	3	9
3	5	8	4
9	8	9	5

❬?❭ ANSWER NO. 188 ❬?❭

PUZZLE 130

Scales 1 and 2 are in perfect balance. If one C is the same as four As, how many As are needed to balance the third set?

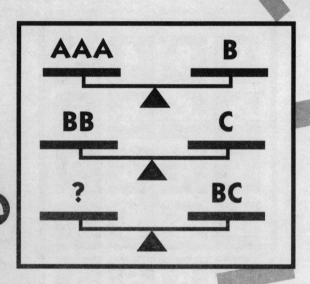

ANSWER NO. 127

PUZZLE 131

How many rectangles of any size can
you find in this diagram?

? ANSWER NO.7 ?

PUZZLE 132

Which squares contain the same numbers?

	A	B	C	D
1	9 4 3	8 7 6	3 8 4	8 2 3
2	1 2 7	9 6 5	9 2 5	5 8 6
3	5 7 8	5 9 2	4 7 2	8 7 9
4	5 2 9	9 8 1	4 9 2	3 1 8

◆ ANSWER NO. 140 ◆

PUZZLE 133

Use either add, subtract, multiply or divide to give the number shown on the calculator. The same number must be used twice. What is the number?

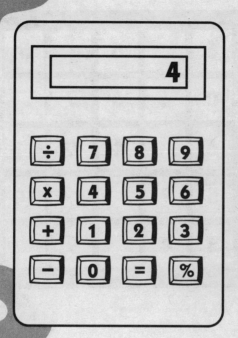

LEVEL D

ANSWER NO.92

PUZZLE 134

Fill in the empty boxes so that every line adds up to 20. What number should replace the question mark?

MIND NUMBING

6		6		5
0	6	6	7	
6		4	0	
5	?			10
3	4		9	

◆?◆ ANSWER NO.67 ◆?◆

PUZZLE 135

Copy out these shapes carefully and rearrange them
to form a number. What is it?

ANSWER NO.200

PUZZLE 136

Which number should replace the question mark to continue the series?

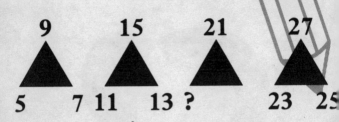

9   15   21   27

5   7 11 13 ?   23 25

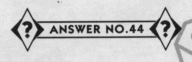 ANSWER NO.44

MIND NUMBING

PUZZLE 137

Here is a series of numbers. Which number should replace the question mark?

| ? | 128 | 64 | 32 | 16 | 8 | 4 |

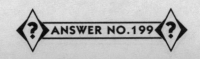 ANSWER NO.199

PUZZLE 138

The number 110 zaps this spaceship. Add together the numbers found on it and multiply the total by either 2, 3, 4, 5, 6, or 7. Which number ought you to use?

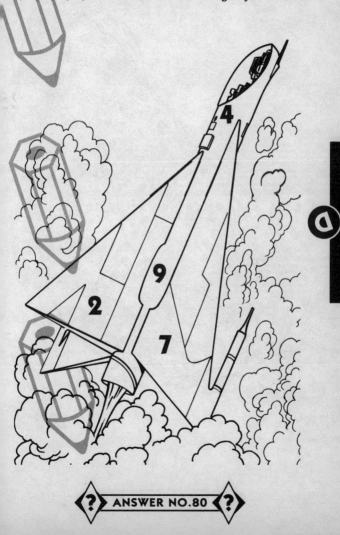

ANSWER NO.80

PUZZLE 139

How many 9's can be found in this
Tyrannosaurus Rex?

MIND NUMBING

ANSWER NO.164

Find the correct six numbers to put in the frame.
There are two choices for each square, for example
1A would give the number 2. When the correct
numbers have been found an easy series will appear.
What is the series?

	1	2	3	4
A	2	1	7	21
B	15	17	6	18
C	1	4	11	10
D	3	4	17	19

LEVEL D

2A	4B	3B	4C	3A	4A
3D	1D	1A	2D	1B	2C

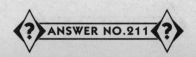

? ANSWER NO.211 ?

PUZZLE 141

Which of the numbers in the square is the odd one out and why?

? ANSWER NO.56 ?

PUZZLE 142

Join together the dots using only those numbers that can be divided by 10. Start at the lowest and discover the object. What is it?

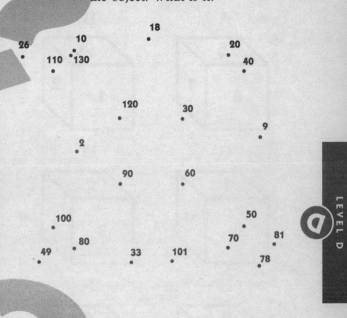

ANSWER NO.128

PUZZLE 143

Which of these pictures is not of the same box?

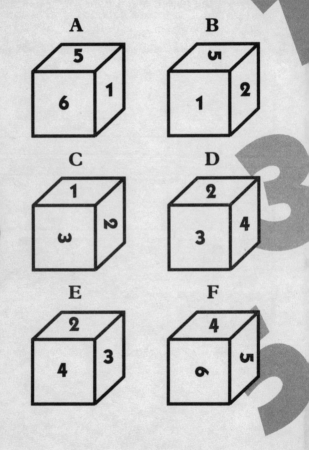

A

B

C

D

E

F

ANSWER NO.116

PUZZLE 144

Fill up this square with the numbers 1 to 5 so that no row, column or diagonal line of five squares uses the same number more than once. What number should replace the question mark?

PUZZLE 145

Each slice of this cake has a number written on it. Using the numbers shown how many different ways are there to add four numbers together to make a total of 12? A number can be used more than once, but a group cannot be repeated in a different order.

PUZZLE 146

Look at the pattern of numbers in the diagram. What number should replace the question mark?

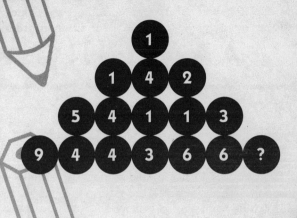

E

AAARGH!

★ LEVEL E ★

PUZZLE 147

The numbers in the middle section have some connection with those down the sides. Find out what it is and tell us what should replace the question mark?

8	2	4
6	3	2
9	3	3
7	7	1
4	?	2

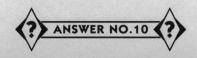

ANSWER NO.10

PUZZLE 148

Move up or across from the bottom left-hand 8 to the top right-hand 7. Collect nine numbers and add them together. What is the lowest you can score?

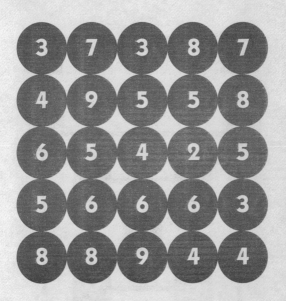

PUZZLE 149

Start at any corner and follow the lines. Add up
the first four numbers you meet and then add on the
corner number. How many different routes will add
up to 21?

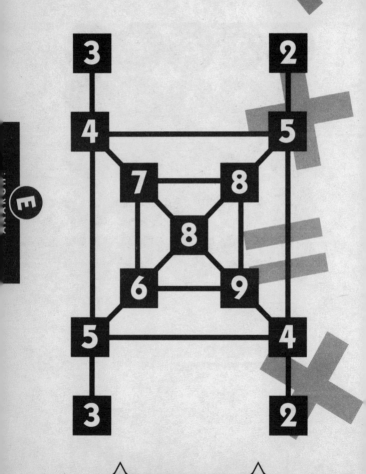

ANSWER NO.57

PUZZLE 150

Place in the middle box a number larger than 1.
If the number is the correct one, all the other numbers
can be divided by it without leaving any remainder.
What is the number?

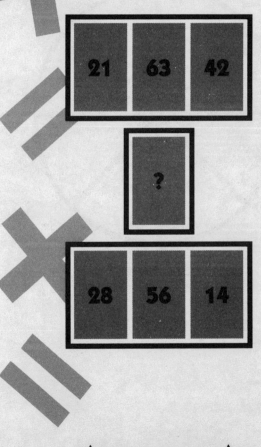

ANSWER NO.81

PUZZLE 151

Each sector of the circle follows a pattern.
What number should replace the question mark?

PUZZLE 152

Here is an unusual safe. Each of the buttons must be
pressed only once in the correct order to open it. The
last button is marked F. The number of moves and
the direction is marked on each button. Thus 1i would
mean one move in, whilst 1O would mean one move
out. 1C would mean one move clockwise and 1A
would mean one move anti-clockwise. Which button is
the first you must press?
Here's a clue: look on the inner circle.

ANSWER NO.34

PUZZLE 153

Each slice of this cake adds up to the same number. Also each ring of the cake totals the same. Which number should appear in the blanks?

ANSWER NO.21

PUZZLE 154

If you look carefully you should see why the numbers are written as they are. What number should replace the question mark?

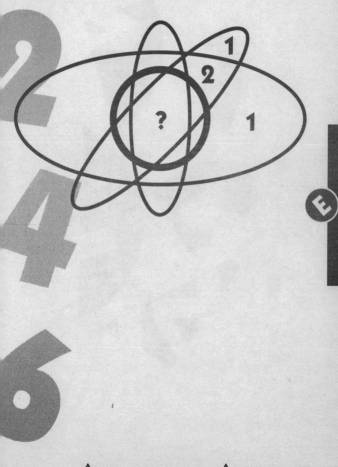

ANSWER NO.22

PUZZLE 155

Copy the cake slices out carefully and rearrange them to find the birthday. How old were the twins?

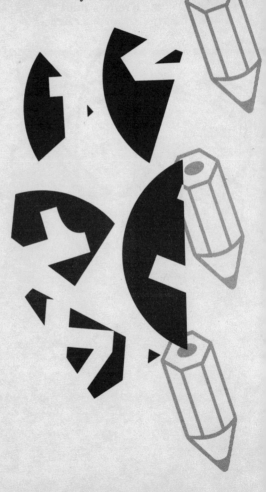

ANSWER NO.178

PUZZLE 156

Start at the A and move to B passing through various parts of the cow. There is a number in each part and these must be added together. What is the lowest number you can total?

LEVEL E

ANSWER NO. 70

PUZZLE 157

Each sector of this wheel has a number written on it. Using the numbers shown how many different ways are there to add four numbers together to make a total of 14? A number can be used more than once, but a group cannot be repeated in a different order.

AAARGH!

E

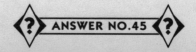ANSWER NO.45

PUZZLE 158

Move from the bottom left-hand 8 to the top right-hand 5 adding together all five numbers. Each black circle is worth minus 4 and this should be taken away from your total each time you meet one. What is the lowest total and how many different routes are there to find it?

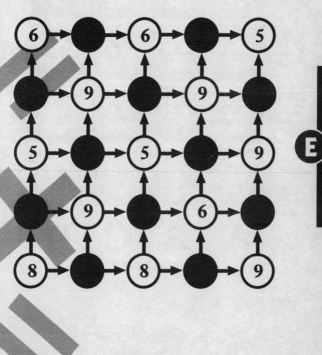

ANSWER NO.93

LEVEL E

E

PUZZLE 159

The numbers in column D are linked in some way to
those in A, B and C. What number should replace
the question mark?

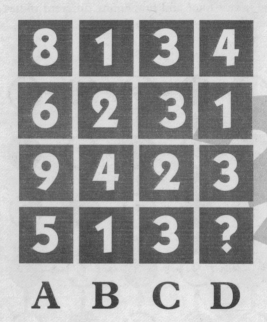

A B C D

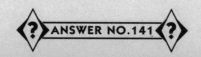

PUZZLE 160

Each symbol is worth a number. The total of the symbols can be found alongside each row and column. What number should replace the question mark?

ANSWER NO.189

PUZZLE 161

On the planet Venox the coins used are 1V, 2V, 5V, 10V, 20V and 50V. A Venoxian has 2,349V in his squiggly bank. He has the same number of five kinds of coin. How many of each are there and what are they?

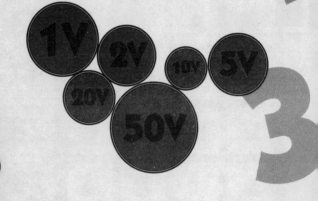

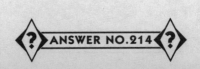

ANSWER NO.214

PUZZLE 162

Replace each question mark with either plus, minus, multiply or divide. Each sign can be used more than once. When the correct ones have been used the sum will be completed. What are the signs?

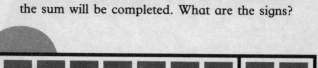

ANSWER NO.105

PUZZLE 163

Which number should replace the question mark to continue the series?

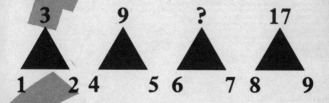

ANSWER NO.46

LEVEL E

PUZZLE 164

What is the lowest number of lines needed to divide the bear so that you can find the numbers 1, 2, 3, 4, 5 and 6 in each section?

ANSWER NO.106

PUZZLE 165

Follow the arrows and find the longest possible route.
How many boxes have been entered?

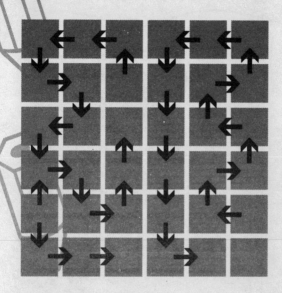

PUZZLE 166

The symbol on the flag will give a number. What is it?

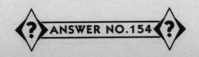

ANSWER NO.154

PUZZLE 167

Start at the middle 5 and move from circle to touching circle. Collect three numbers and add them to the 5. How many different routes are there to make a total of 16?

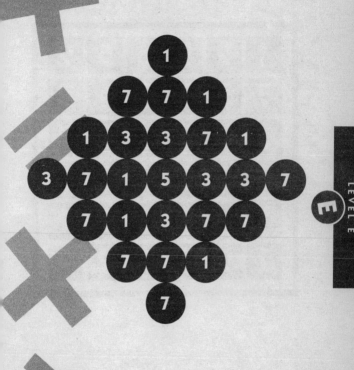

LEVEL E

PUZZLE 168

Divide up the box into six identical shapes. The
numbers in each shape add up to the same.
How is this done?

PUZZLE 169

Scales 1 and 2 are in perfect balance.
How many Cs are needed to balance the third set?

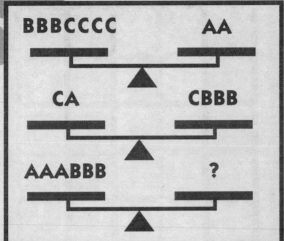

BBBCCCC   AA

CA   CBBB

AAABBB   ?

LEVEL E

ANSWER NO. 129

PUZZLE 170

How many squares of any size can you find in
this diagram?

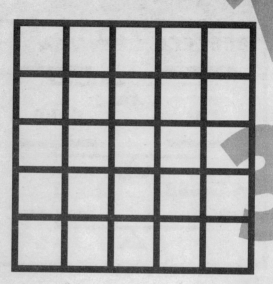

AAARGH!

PUZZLE 171

Which squares contain the same numbers?

	A	B	C	D	E
1	4 7 / 4 8	2 / 2 1	1 / 3 8 / 9	1 / 5 9 / 3	7 7 / 1 8
2	3 1 / 2	8 / 8 8	4 3 / 2 1	3 3 / 4 4	2 3 / 9 1
3	8 2 / 1 4	5 / 6 8 / 7	3 9 / 4 5	9 9 / 9 9	6 / 7 8 / 7
4	5 / 6 6 / 5	2 / 3 3	7 1 / 8 7	5 5 / 6 1	1 / 5 2 / 3
5	1 7 / 7 8	9 / 8 8 / 1	6 7 / 6 7	6 / 4 1 / 5	4 4 / 2 2

LEVEL E

? ANSWER NO. 142 ?

PUZZLE 172

What is the least number of buttons you must press to turn the number shown on the calculator into 17?

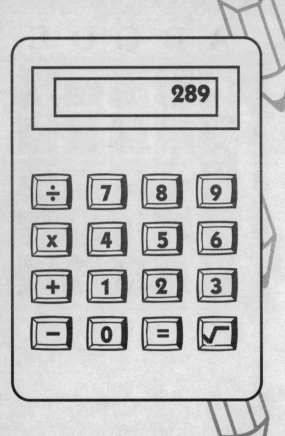

❓ ANSWER NO.94 ❓

AAARGH!

PUZZLE 173

Fill in the empty boxes, using two numbers only, so
that every line adds up to 25.
What number should replace the question mark?

	6	?	0	5
				0
5		5	3	5
	3	3	3	12
5	2	3	12	3

ANSWER NO.69

PUZZLE 174

Copy out these shapes carefully and rearrange
them to form a number. What is it?

AAARGH!

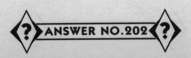

PUZZLE 175

To zap the spaceship find the number which, when multiplied by itself, will equal the total of the numbers shown. What is the number?

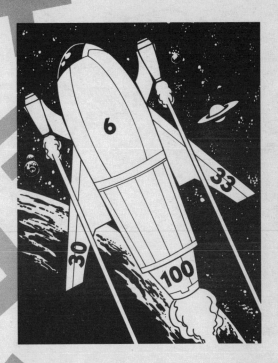

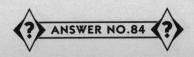
ANSWER NO.84

LEVEL E

PUZZLE 176

How many 2's can be found in this Triceratops?

PUZZLE 177

Find the correct six numbers to put in the frame.
There are two choices for each square, for example
1A would give the number 22. When the correct
numbers have been found a series will appear.
What is the series?

	1	2	3	4	5
A	22	24	16	3	9
B	6	62	15	30	12
C	40	27	36	70	35
D	60	18	7	11	4
E	8	72	13	28	48

1C	2A	3C	2C	1D	2E
5B	4D	5A	5E	4E	3B

ANSWER NO.213

PUZZLE 178

Which of the numbers in the square is the odd one out and why?

42	15	63	6
9	81	33	21
96	16	12	48
18	60	3	90

AAARGH!

ANSWER NO.58

PUZZLE 179

Join together the dots using only those numbers that
can be divided by 5. Start at the lowest and discover
the object. What is it?

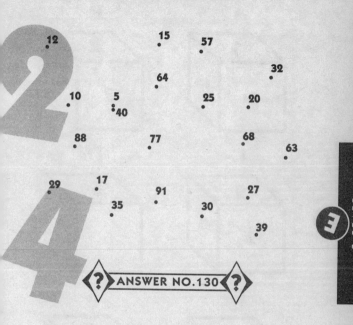

ANSWER NO.130

LEVEL E

PUZZLE 180

Here is a series of numbers.
Which number should replace the question mark?

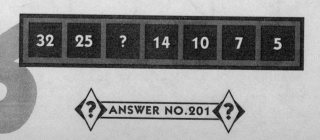

| 32 | 25 | ? | 14 | 10 | 7 | 5 |

ANSWER NO.201

PUZZLE 181

Which of these pictures is not of the same box?

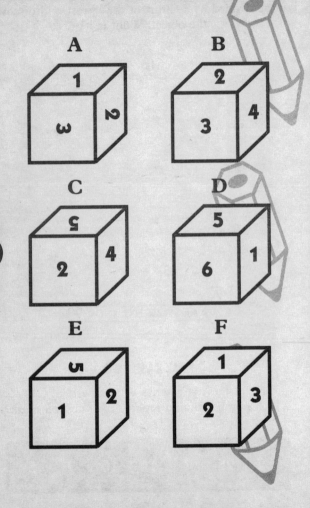

A

1
2
3

B

2
4
3

C

5
4
2

D

5
1
6

E

5
2
1

F

1
3
2

? ANSWER NO.118 ?

AAARGH!

PUZZLE 182

Fill up this square with the numbers 1 to 5 so that no row, column or diagonal line of five squares uses the same number more than once. What number should replace the question mark?

ANSWER NO.50

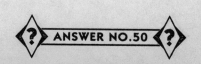

PUZZLE 183

Look at the pattern of numbers in the diagram. What number should replace the question mark?

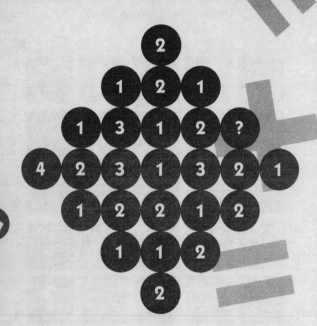

ANSWER NO.165

SUPER GENIUS

★ LEVEL F ★

PUZZLE 184

The numbers in the middle section have some connection with those down the sides. Find out what it is and tell us what should replace the question mark?

3	51	5
8	46	8
2	41	7
3	21	4
6	?	9

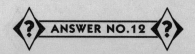

? ANSWER NO.12 ?

PUZZLE 185

Move up or across from the bottom left-hand 5 to the top right-hand 3. Collect nine numbers and add them together. What is the highest you can score?

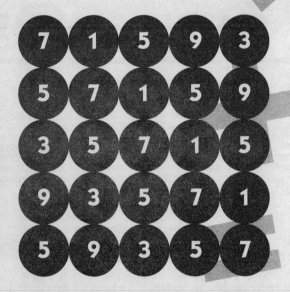

ANSWER NO.179

PUZZLE 186

Start at any corner and follow the lines. Add up the
first four numbers you meet and then add on the
corner number. What is the lowest possible total
and how many different routes lead to it?

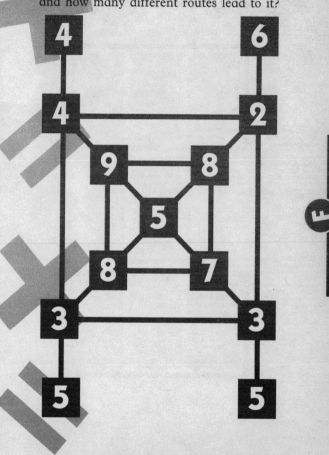

LEVEL F

? ANSWER NO.59 ?

PUZZLE 187

Place in the middle box a number larger than 1.
If the number is the correct one, all the other numbers
can be divided by it without leaving any remainder.
What is the number?

F

ANSWER NO.83

PUZZLE 188

Each sector of the circle follows a pattern.
What number should replace the question mark?

ANSWER NO.155

LEVEL F

PUZZLE 189

Here is an unusual safe. Each of the buttons must be
pressed only once in the correct order to open it. The
last button is marked F. The number of moves and
the direction is marked on each button. Thus 1i would
mean one move in, whilst 1O would mean one move
out. 1C would mean one move clockwise and 1A
would mean one move anti-clockwise.
Which button is the first you must press?
Here's a clue: look on the outer rim.

PUZZLE 190

Each slice of this cake adds up to the same number.
Also each ring of the cake totals the same. Which 2
numbers should appear in the blanks?

PUZZLE 191

Copy the cake slices out carefully and rearrange them to find the birthday. How old was the birthday girl?

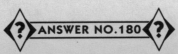

ANSWER NO.180

PUZZLE 192

Start at the A and move to B passing through the various parts of the duck. There is a number in each part and these must be added together. What is the lowest number you can total?

LEVEL F

‹?› ANSWER NO.72 ‹?›

PUZZLE 193

If you look carefully you should see why the numbers are written as they are. What number should replace the question mark?

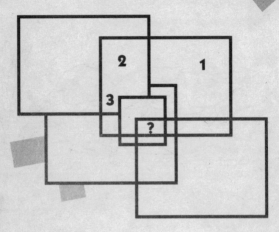

F

ANSWER NO.24

PUZZLE 194

Move from the bottom left-hand 6 to the top
right-hand 7 adding together all five numbers.
Each black circle is worth minus 5 and this should be
taken away from your total each time you meet one.
How many different routes, each giving a total of 10,
can be found?

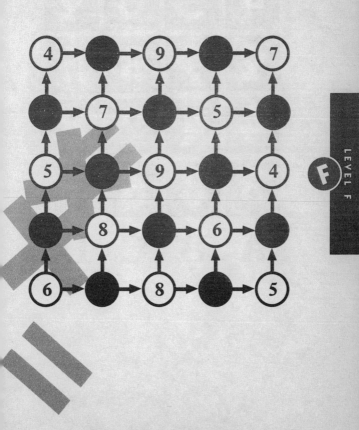

ANSWER NO.95

PUZZLE 195

The numbers in column D are linked in some way to those in A, B and C. What number should replace the question mark?

A	B	C	D
4	3	6	2
2	9	3	6
4	4	2	8
3	8	6	?

ANSWER NO.143

PUZZLE 196

Each symbol is worth a number. The total of the symbols can be found alongside a row and two columns. What number should replace the question mark?

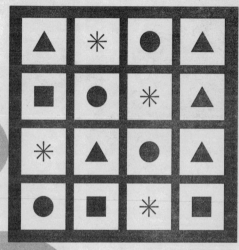

85

? 50 45

ANSWER NO.191

PUZZLE 197

On the planet Venox the coins used are 1V, 2V, 5V,
10V, 20V and 50V. A Venoxian has 3,071V in his
squiggly bank. He has the same number of five kinds
of coin. How many of each are there and
what are they?

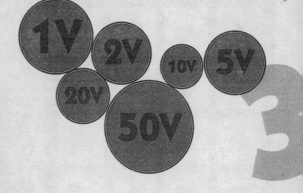

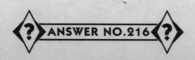ANSWER NO.216

PUZZLE 198

What is the lowest number of lines needed to divide the cat so that the numbers in each section always total 17?

LEVEL F

ANSWER NO. 108

PUZZLE 199

Replace each question mark with either plus, minus,
multiply or divide. Each sign can be used more than
once. When the correct ones have been used
the sum will be completed. What are the signs?

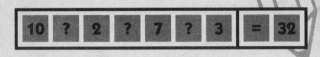

| 10 | ? | 2 | ? | 7 | ? | 3 | | = | 32 |

ANSWER NO.107

PUZZLE 200

The symbol on the flag will give a number.
What is it?

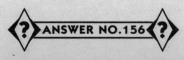
ANSWER NO.156

PUZZLE 201

Follow the arrows and find the longest possible route.
How many boxes have been entered?

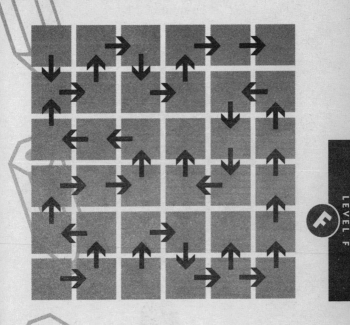

LEVEL F

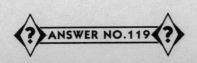

PUZZLE 202

Start at the middle 9 and move from circle to touching circle. Collect three numbers and add them to the 9. How many different routes are there to make a total of 17?

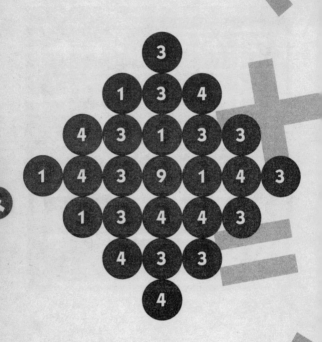

ANSWER NO.35

PUZZLE 203

Divide up the box into four identical shapes. The
numbers in each shape add up to the same.
How is this done?

LEVEL F

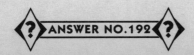
ANSWER NO. 192

PUZZLE 204

Scales 1 and 2 are in perfect balance.
How many Bs are needed to balance the third set?

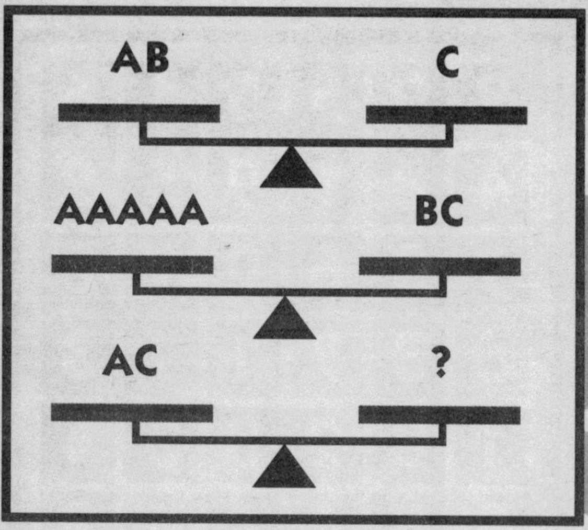

AB — C

AAAAA — BC

AC — ?

F

ANSWER NO. 131

PUZZLE 205

How many rectangles of any size can you find in this diagram?

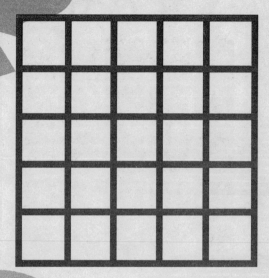

PUZZLE 206

Which squares contain the same numbers?

	A	B	C	D	E
1	3 4 6 9	1 8 3 8	2 6 4 8	1 2 3 4	1 6 3 9
2	5 1 3 5	9 1 2 8	2 3 3 2	1 3 9 7	5 5 6 5 5
3	1 3 9 6	1 4 7 8	4 4 3 3	6 3 9 1	1 5 9 8
4	7 7 6 6	6 7 8 9	9 9 8 2	9 9 9 1	9 6 4 8
5	4 6 3 7	8 2 3 4	3 1 6 9	4 4 6 9	8 8 8 8

SUPER GENIUS F

PUZZLE 207

How many ways are there to score 25 on this
dartboard using four darts only? Each dart always
lands in a segment and no dart falls to the floor. Once
a group of numbers has been used it cannot be
repeated in a different order.

ANSWER NO.47

LEVEL F

PUZZLE 208

Fill in the empty boxes so that every line adds up to 30. Use two numbers only, one of which is double the other. What number should replace the question mark?

	6		1	7
5				1
		6		
	?			14
5			13	

ANSWER NO. 71

PUZZLE 209

Here is a series of numbers.
Which number should replace the question mark?

| 49 | 7 | 9 | 3 | 64 | 8 | 25 | ? |

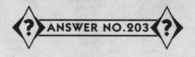
⟨?⟩ ANSWER NO.203 ⟨?⟩

PUZZLE 210

Which number should replace the question mark to
continue the series?

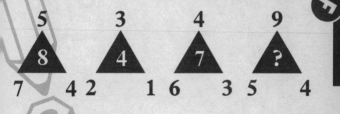

5   3   4   9
  8   4   7   ?
7   4 2   1 6   3 5   4

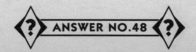
⟨?⟩ ANSWER NO.48 ⟨?⟩

PUZZLE 211

To zap the spaceship find the number which, when multiplied by itself, will equal the total of the numbers shown. What is the number?

SUPER GENIUS

ANSWER NO.82

PUZZLE 212

How many 8's can be found in this Brontosaurus?

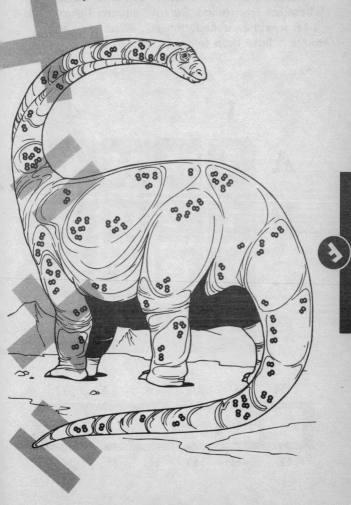

ANSWER NO.168

PUZZLE 213

Find the correct six numbers to put in the frame.
There are two choices for each square, for example
1A would give the number 7. When the correct
numbers have been found an easy series will appear.
What is the series?

	1	2	3	4
A	7	16	11	4
B	1	12	18	3
C	9	13	8	14
D	5	2	17	2

4D	2C	4A	1A	3A	3D
1B	4B	1D	3C	1C	2C

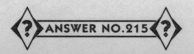

ANSWER NO. 215

PUZZLE 214

Which two numbers on the square do not
fit the pattern and why?

3	17	11	9
5	15	7	13
12	8	1	19
2	10	16	4

ANSWER NO.60

PUZZLE 215

Join together the dots using only those numbers that can be divided by 4. Start at the lowest and discover the object. What is it?

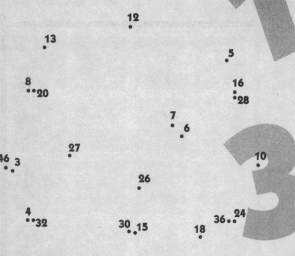

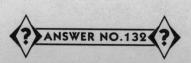
ANSWER NO. 132

PUZZLE 216

Copy out these shapes carefully and rearrange
them to form a number. What is it?

ANSWER NO.204

PUZZLE 217

Which of these pictures are not of the same box?

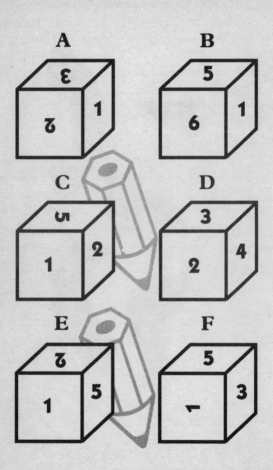

? ANSWER NO.120 ?

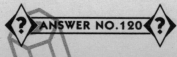

PUZZLE 218

Fill up this square with the numbers 1 to 5 so that no row, column or diagonal line of five squares uses the same number more than once.
What number should replace the question mark?

LEVEL F

PUZZLE 219

Look at the pattern of number in the diagram.
What number should replace the question mark?

ANSWERS

1   14.

2   8. The numbers down the sides are placed together in the middle section.

3   30.

4   19. The numbers down the sides are placed together in the middle section in reverse order.

5   36.

6   11. The numbers down the sides are added together to give the number in the middle section.

7   100.

8   6. The number down the right-hand side is taken from the the number down the left-hand side to give the number in the middle section.

9   55.

10   2. The number down the left-hand side is divided by the number down the right-hand side to give the number in the middle section.

11 225.

12 45. The numbers down the sides are multiplied together to give the number in the middle section, placed in a reversed order.

13 3.

14 1. The number is surrounded by only one shape.

15 2 in the outer section and 4 in the inner one.

16 3. The number is found in 3 overlapping shapes.

17 8 in the outer section at the top, 3 in the outer section below and 5 in the inner one.

18 3. The number is found in 3 overlapping shapes.

19 2.

20 3. The number is found in 3 overlapping shapes.

21 9.

22 4. The number is found in 4 overlapping shapes.

23 4 and 6.

24 4. The number is found in 4 overlapping shapes.

25 4.

26 2D, in the third column.

27 7.

28	1R.	42	6. Move from triangle to triangle, beginning on the left, to read 1, 2, 3, 4. Start again to get 5, 6, 7, 8. Then move to the top to get 9, 10, 11, 12.
29	6.		
30	2S, in the fourth column.		
31	10.		
32	1i, found between 4A and 3C.	43	7.
33	13.	44	17. Odd numbers increase in order from left, to right, to top around each triangle.
34	1C.		
35	12.		
36	1C.	45	23.
37	9.	46	13. The two numbers at the base of each triangle are added to give the top number.
38	8.		
39	8.		
40	9.	47	22.
41	8.		

48 10. The left-hand number is added to the top number and then the right-hand number is subtracted to give the centre number.

49 42.

50 3.

51 14.

52 7. It is the only odd number.

53 23.

54 32. It is the only even number.

55 23.

56 14. All the other numbers are divisible by 4.

57 4.

58 16. All the other numbers are divisible by 3.

59 16 is the lowest and there are 2 routes.

60 Each pair of numbers on each row total 20. The first two on the bottom row, 2 and 10, do not.

61 1.

62 11.

63 2.

64 12.

65 0 and 6.

66 10.

67 1.

68 27.

69 7.

70	31.	84	13.
71	4.	85	19.
72	13.	86	Times and 2.
73	2.	87	30.
74	4.	88	8, times and 8.
75	3.	89	20.
76	19.	90	12.
77	5.	91	18.
78	2.	92	2. 2 times 2 or 2 plus 2.
79	11.		
80	5.	93	13 and one way.
81	7.	94	1. Square root.($\sqrt{}$)
82	12.	95	5.
83	13.	96	3.
		97	Plus and plus.

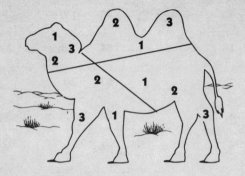

99 Plus and minus.

100 3.

101 Minus, times and
plus.

102 3.

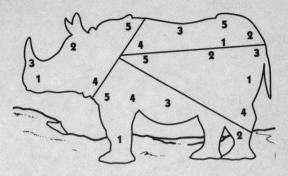

103 Multiply, plus and minus.

104 4.

105 Plus, divide and
multiply.

106 4.

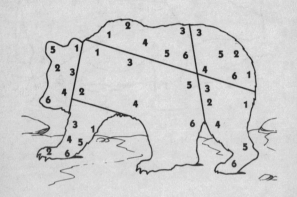

107 Divide, multiply
and minus.

108 4.

109	18.	**125**	6.
110	C.	**126**	A Star.
111	13.	**127**	9.
112	F.	**128**	A Maltese Cross.
113	16.	**129**	16.
114	B.	**130**	An arrow.
115	17.	**131**	2.
116	E.	**132**	An envelope.
117	17.	**133**	6. Add together A, B and C to get D.
118	F.		
119	19.	**134**	1A and 3C.
120	D and E.	**135**	9. Add together A, B and C in order to get D.
121	6.		
122	A hammer.	**136**	1B and 4D.
123	2.	**137**	7. Add together A, B and C to get D.
124	A tent.		

138 3B and 1D.

139 6. Add together A and B, then take away C in order to get D.

140 2C, 3B and 4A.

141 1. A minus B minus C gives D.

142 1E, 4C and 5A.

143 4. A times B divided by C gives D.

144 1E, 3A, 3D and 5C.

145 3. Each sector contains the numbers 1, 2 and 3.

146 3. A 3 and its mirror image are placed together.

147 23. The numbers 1 to 24 are contained in the sectors.

148 7. A 7 and its mirror image are placed together.

149 2. The numbers in each sector total 12.

150 4. A 4 and its mirror image are placed together.

151 1. Each sector's total increases by 1.

152 2. A 2 and its mirror image are placed together top and bottom.

153 3. Opposite sectors total the same.

154 3. A 3, on its side, and its mirror image are placed together.

155 9. Each sector in the bottom half of the circle totals double its opposite.

156 5. A 5 and its mirror image are placed together.

157 1. The pattern is symmetrical.

158 10.

159 2. The pattern is symmetrical.

160 26.

161 4. The total of each horizontal line increases by 1.

162 30.

163 9. Each column of numbers totals 9.

164 65.

165 1. The total of each horizontal line doubles from the outside to the centre.

166 40.

167 4. The total of each horizontal line doubles from the outside to the centre.

168 97.

169 12.

170 10.

ANSWERS

171 15.

172 7.

173 41.

174 21.

175 15.

176 5.

177 50.

178 14.

179 47.

180 12.

181 8.

182

2	5	5	9
8	9	2	5
5	8	9	2
9	2	8	8

183 9.

184

7	3	3	7
6	4	6	4
3	6	3	7
4	7	6	4

185 22.

186

1	6	1	2	4
6	6	4	6	1
2	4	2	1	6
4	2	6	6	2
6	1	6	4	6

187 21.

188

9	8	4	3
3	5	8	5
4	4	3	9
3	5	8	4
9	8	9	5

189 30.

190

1	2	2	5	5	2
7	5	7	3	1	3
3	9	9	1	9	7
9	3	7	1	3	5
1	5	2	3	7	1
7	2	9	5	2	9

191 60.

192

2	9	5	5	1	6
4	8	1	9	5	2
7	3	6	2	7	8
6	3	7	1	7	3
1	8	2	8	3	4
9	5	4	4	6	9

193 3. The series reads
1, 2, 3,
1, 2, 3, etc.

194 4.

195 28. The numbers
increase
by 4 each time.

196 3.

197 16. The numbers
increase by
3 each time.

198 5.

199 256. The numbers
halve from the left
each time.

200 8.

201 19. The series of
numbers decreases
from the left by 7,
then 6, then 5,
then 4, etc.

202 2.

203 5. Each number
has its square root
placed next to it.

204 5.

205 1 2 3 4 5 6. The numbers increase by 1 each time.

206 5 of 2V, 5V and 10V coins.

207 2 4 6 8 10 12. The numbers increase by 2 each time.

208 22 of 2V, 5V and 10V coins.

209 1 3 5 7 9 11. The numbers increase by 2 each time.

210 17 of 1V, 2V, 5V and 10V coins.

211 1 3 6 10 15 21. The numbers increase by 2, 3, 4, etc.

212 31 of 1V, 2V, 5V and 10V coins.

213 12 24 36 48 60 72. The numbers increase by 12 each time.

214 27 of 2V, 5V, 10V, 20V and 50V coins.

215 2 3 5 7 11 13. These are all prime numbers.

216 37 of 1V, 2V, 10V, 20V and 50V coins.

217 5.

218 2.

219 4.